GOSLING, Ted
Around Seaton and Beer
942.357

IMAGES OF ENGLAND

AROUND SEATON AND BEER

TED GOSLING

TEMPUS

Dedicated to my first granddaughter, Tallulah, who I know will help me to unlock rooms in my mind I had long forgotten.

Frontispiece: A charming picture of Seaton Hole taken in 1890. Before 1871 most Victorians went to the beach only for their health but the Bank Holiday Act of 1871 led to many social changes and gave seaside towns a new lease of life. Seaton enjoyed an increasing influx of summer visitors, and when they arrived at the resort they found a variety of apartments and newly built hotels to accommodate their needs. *E.S. Gosling collection*

First published 2003

Tempus Publishing Limited
The Mill, Brimscombe Port,
Stroud, Gloucestershire, GL5 2QG
www.tempus-publishing.com

© Ted Gosling, 2003

The right of Ted Gosling to be identified as the Author
of this work has been asserted in accordance with the
Copyrights, Designs and Patents Act 1988.

British Library Cataloguing in Publication Data.
A catalogue record for this book is available from the British Library.

ISBN 0 7524 3052 1

Typesetting and origination by Tempus Publishing Limited.
Printed in Great Britain by Midway Colour Print, Wiltshire.

Contents

The East Walk, Seaton, 1895. The ruthless pace at which we live today is so different from the leisurely world of Victorian Seaton. *E.S. Gosling collection*

Introduction

The arrival of the railways transformed the villages and towns around Seaton, since the very equable sea breezes and climate brought Victorians to the district for bathing and their holidays. Hitherto, Seaton was a small coastal village with, yes, an even smaller population than Beer right up to the early 1960s. The combined parish has a long history dating back centuries, but even so it is difficult to visualise the hard times that its inhabitants had to endure in the past.

Views had been painted by visiting artists but the invention of the camera brought a new dimension to illustrating pictorially what is now very much part of the Axe Valley's heritage.

Ted Gosling is a true Seaton boy who involved himself in local affairs during the Second World War, belonging to the Scouts, and acting as a messenger boy in the event of an air raid. He developed an interest in collecting old photographs and documents of Seaton and its immediately neighbouring villages. His interest in local history and the collection of photographs he amassed led him to set up displays and exhibitions to the benefit of the neighbourhood. Ted has done this now for over fifty years. His knowledge of the local area is legendary and led him to become a founder of the Seaton Museum, for which he has been the Honorary Curator since its inauguration. The interest in Ted's collection is now secure in the form of the Axe Valley Heritage Association and is on permanent display at Seaton for future generations to enjoy.

This latest addition to the collection of books Ted has written and illustrated draws our attention to the changing times in which we live in our beloved East Devon. It is an excellent addition of a generation or two of those who are still remembered and many recognised in surroundings we enjoy. These could so easily be forgotten without the foresight of this local Seaton boy half a century ago.

Norman Lambert
Beer 2003

It was a fine summer's day in 1899 when the Seaton photographer George Barton took this picture of the old Beer road at Seaton. Although fine buildings were already disappearing in this area at that time, nothing else had yet happened to disturb the tranquillity of the countryside. In the late nineteenth century, Seaton was still rural. Properties such as these would have attracted middle-class Victorian families. *E.S. Gosling collection*

Acknowledgements

I am grateful to all those donors who, over the past fifty years, have given photographs and postcards to add to my collection.

I am indeed indebted to Norman Lambert for his introduction and his help, and to Ron Durrans for pictures he sent to Seaton Museum regarding his stay in Seaton as a young man.

Thanks must go to Tony and Mary Byrne-Jones who recorded events over the past fifty years.

Particular thanks must go to Heather Sanham without whose help the book would not have been possible. I am also grateful to my wife Carol and the staff at Tempus for their assistance with this book.

I have given the photographs in my collection to Seaton Museum, to safeguard them for future generations to enjoy.

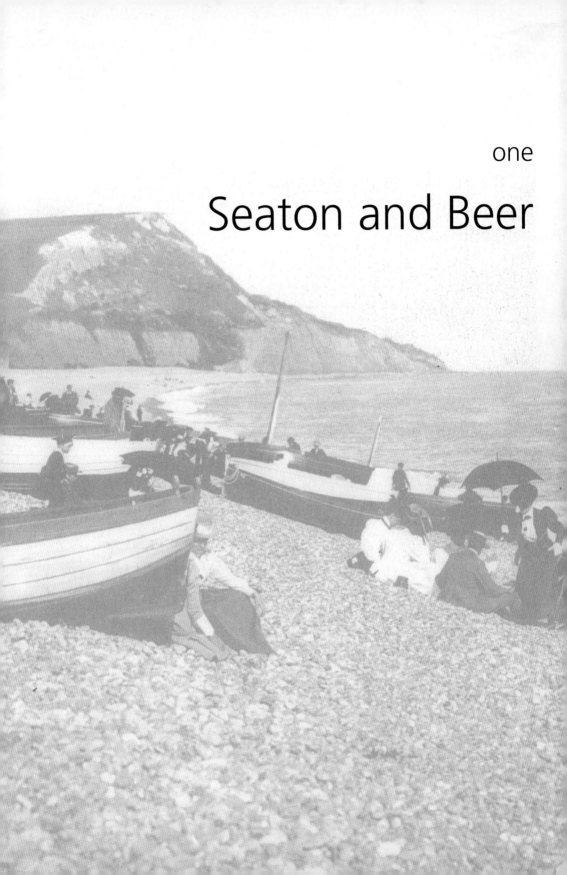

one

Seaton and Beer

The Manor Farm Dairy, *c.* 1901. This thatched property stood next to the old primary school in Fore Street, and was demolished in the early 1960s. At the time of this picture, a dairy belonging to W.H. Aplin operated from here. *E.S. Gosling collection*

Violet Terrace, 1895. Views of houses that no longer exist seem to be magical. In them, the vanished past is switched back on and the past is made present again. Violet Terrace was demolished in the early 1970s to make way for the present Windsor Gardens but here, on a full summer's day, long hot and lazy, the Terrace can be seen in all its Victorian splendour. *E.S. Gosling collection*

A poor-quality but interesting photograph of Marine Crescent taken around 1890. At that time the houses in Marine Crescent were nearly all run as apartments with Mrs Henry Abbott at No. 8, Miss Effie Major at No. 6 and Mary Ann Welch at No. 5. This form of boarding-house was nearly always run by the lady of the house. This was taken before the Westleigh was built, and the house seen on the far right was part of the Bath House. *E.S. Gosling collection*

Looking up Fore Street, *c.* 1921. Goulds Restaurant and confectionery establishment traded in the shop now occupied by Woolworths. Wedding breakfasts, balls and luncheons were catered for by Mr Gould in the best possible style; he even advertised American iced drinks, which must have been a novelty for Seaton people in those days. Note the attractive appearance of the properties on the left side of the picture before they were spoiled by shop fronts. *E.S. Gosling collection*

Looking up Fore Street, 1885. Photography was still sufficiently unusual to attract attention and these people of Victorian Seaton were caught staring earnestly at the photographer. Prospect House, in the left of the foreground, was then occupied by J. Turner and Co. Wine Vaults, and you can see by the state of the road that the horse still ruled supreme. *E.S. Gosling collection*

Seaton Esplanade, 1875. At this time fishing was a major industry in the town and the beach was a busy place, packed with fishing boats. The bathhouse seen in the left foreground provided both residents and visitors with hot and cold sea water baths. It was run by the Woodgate family who charged the then exorbitant price of 2s 6d for a hot bath, 2s for a tepid bath and 1s for a cold one. *E.S. Gosling collection*

Seaton Beach. By the end of the nineteenth century the seaside holiday had become an annual event for all those who could afford it and here, on a hot summer's day in August 1897, they are enjoying a day on the beach. *E.S. Gosling collection*

Fore Street, 1906. Here, nearly a century ago, some of the good people of Seaton are standing in the middle of the road outside the new Town Hall, looking at the photographer. Anyone who tried that today would be dead or maimed within seconds; in those far-off days the street was still a place where you could stand about and talk. *E.S. Gosling collection*

Looking down Queen Street, 1890. The shop on the left belonged to John Real, who was a greengrocer and a licensed dealer in game. Down on the right, the premises with the cart outside belonged to Diment and Co. They were gas fitters and hot water engineers. Early in the twentieth century, Mr Diment opened the first motor garage in Seaton. The group of ladies in earnest conversation and the errand boy on his bicycle all add to the period charm of this picture. *E.S. Gosling collection*

Seaton Beach and Haven Cliff, 1885. Remains of the old Custom House can be seen at the mouth of the river. You can also note the large building to the left which was then the Axmouth Harbour Warehouse. *E.S. Gosling collection*

Queen Street, Seaton, 1900. Views like this of houses that no longer exist seem to be inherently magical and we are sadly reminded by them how quickly things change. The attractive houses on the left were pulled down, along with the stone buildings on the corner of Beer Road, to be replaced with flats and shops. How much better it all looked then. *E.S. Gosling collection*

SEATON. DEVON

THE ROYAL CLARENCE HOTEL

FULLY LICENCED   R.A.C. A.A.   ON SEA FRONT.

LUNCHEON, TEA and DINNER PARTIES catered for   Phone 15

The Hotel is most cheery and comfortable, and the spacious, dainty COCKTAIL LOUNGE is a most popular rendezvous

THE CUISINE is excellent, and the TERMS MOST REASONABLE.

HOT AND COLD RUNNING WATER IN ALL BEDROOMS.   PROPRIETRESS: MRS. TREGASKIS

Advertisement for the Royal Clarence Hotel, *c.* 1929. *E.S. Gosling Collection*

Queen Street, 1897. The imposing building seen on the right was once known as Brick House. It got its name because, when built in 1824, it was one of the first houses in the town constructed with brick. At the time of this picture it was occupied by a girls' school. Later still it became Ferris and Prescott, the drapers, and at present a part of the building is Seaton Police Station. *E.S. Gosling collection*

This historic photograph was taken in 1859 and shows the training wall built at the beginning of the nineteenth century by John Hallett, lord of the manor of Axmouth. This increased the rate of the river's flow and helped to clear the mouth of pebbles. *E.S. Gosling collection*

Wessiters House, Seaton, pictured here in 1902, was built as a gentleman's residence in 1843, with the surrounding land laid out as parkland, for John Head. At the time of this photograph, it belonged to William Henry Head who was much involved in the local community. Following his death in 1958, the Wessiters estate was sold by his daughter, Muriel. *Seaton Museum*

The formation of the Seaton and District Electric Light Company in the 1920s heralded a new era for the town. The directors of this new venture were Brigadier-General G.B. Smith, Charles Cane, A. Morton Davey, Major-General H.B.H. Wright and Stanley Cooper. The main office of the Seaton and District Electric Light Company is pictured here in 1935. These premises are now occupied by CMC Financial Advisors. *E.S. Gosling collection*

Violet Terrace was named after its builders of the first half of the nineteenth century. The picture here shows the back of the houses which abutted onto Cross Street, and was taken just before the Terrace was demolished in the early 1970s to make way for the present Windsor Gardens.
E.S. Gosling collection

Advertisement for Friedenheim School for Girls, 1903. The school was in a building once known as 'The Brick House'. Part of this house in Queen Street is now occupied by the police station.
E.S. Gosling collection

Construction work on Fosseway Court, Harbour Road, *c.* 1967. *E.S. Gosling collection*

Seaton East Walk, 1892. By the time of this photograph, the commercial possibilities of Seaton had been recognised. A railway line had made the town accessible, and hotels had been built to cater for visitors. Doctors were recommending Seaton in local guides – after all, people like to feel that what they fancy also does them good. *E.S. Gosling collection*

Eyewell Green was constructed in the early 1930s, and until the 1960s had two points of entry. This picture, taken in 1938, shows the bottom house on the left-hand side with the old way in before this section of road was blocked off. *E.S. Gosling collection*

Thanks to East Devon District Council planners, fields, once in an area of outstanding natural beauty, are now covered with large housing estates after an orgy of modernisation. In this picture you can see the Bovis Homes information centre on Harepath Road. These were the people responsible for this huge estate, built over green fields divided by lush hedgerows, to change forever this image of a rural idyll. *E.S. Gosling collection*

Seaton East Walk, 1962. *E.S. Gosling collection*

Seaton, looking east, 1925. *E.S. Gosling collection*

Advertisement from 1901 Seaton Guide showing local furnished apartments. *E.S. Gosling collection*

Seaton Beach, *c.* 1891. *E.S. Gosling collection*

The photographs above and below were taken during the winter months of 1965. The golf links on Haven Cliff were white with snow in the top picture, and the sea wall was still in the future. In the bottom picture you can see the boundary wall of Seafield House on the left-hand side of Seafield Road, with the Jubilee clock in the background. Seafield House was destroyed by a German bomber during the Second World War and the site is now the Jubilee Gardens. *E.S. Gosling collection*

This paraffin engine that gave Seaton its first electricity supply was kept in BenTrevett's Garage and still provided a DC supply to a few properties in Harbour Road up to the early 1950s. *E.S. Gosling collection*

Marine Place, *c.* 1926. The drinking fountain to the right of the foreground was given to the town by a Mr Willans to mark the Diamond Jubilee of Queen Victoria in 1897. It was removed by Seaton Council in the late 1930s and destroyed. Local children were forbidden by their parents to drink from the fountain in case they contracted some terrible disease. *E.S. Gosling collection*

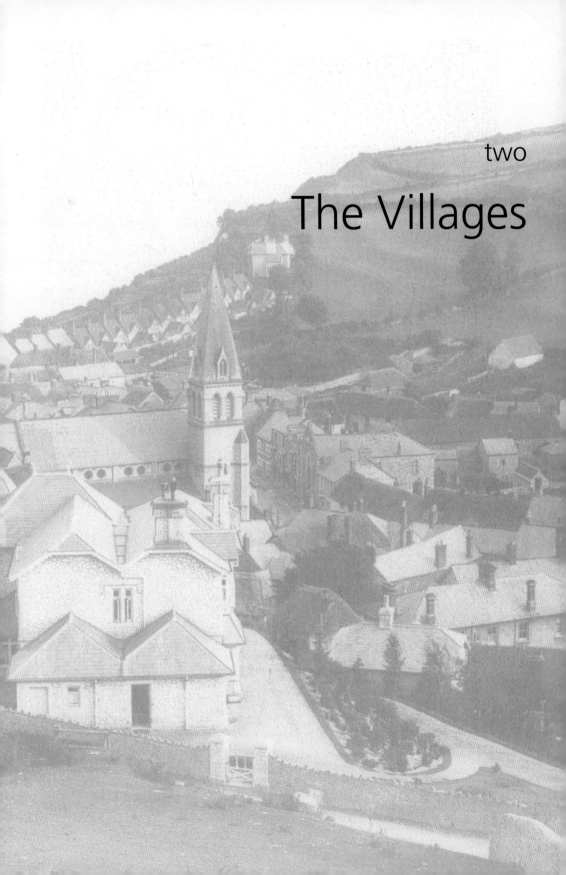

two

The Villages

Beer village, *c.* 1900. East Devon is a colourful patchwork of towns and villages bound together by traditions and dialects. All the locals feel pride in their birthplace, but none more so than the people of Beer who, from the time of this picture to the present day, have always felt a fierce sense of loyalty to their village. This is reflected during Regatta week when Beer welcomes back home the migrants who have settled in other parts of the country, and a great gathering of the clan takes place. *E.S. Gosling collection*

Beer village, *c.* 1895. This extremely detailed view of Beer was taken by a photographer during a visit to Devon in 1895. The photographer was clearly accomplished in his work and in this picture the vanished past is miraculously made present again. At that time, Beer was mainly populated by fishermen, quarrymen and farm workers. Change came slowly to them and the old village ways still remained. The folk of Beer then, as now, were warm-hearted people and strangers were always made welcome. *E.S. Gosling collection*

Opposite below: Shepherd's Cottage, Beer, *c.* 1900. In the background is the shop belonging to Mr A. Northcott. The open stream flowing down one side of the main street is known as The Brook. This brook, supplied with water from a spring near Bovey House, has never been known to run dry and no local-born boy worth his salt can be called a Beer boy until he has fallen into it. *E.S. Gosling collection*

The old chapel of rest at Beer, *c.* 1865. Attached to Seaton's parish church, this chapel of rest was demolished in 1875 and replaced with the present St Michael's church. The nave of the chapel dated from Norman times, although the aisle in the Perpendicular style dates from the fifteenth century. The shop on the left later became a cottage and was pulled down to make way for the Mariners Hall. *E.S. Gosling collection*

Bovey House, Beer, 23 August 1877. A strange, atmospheric photograph of this fine old mansion which was for many years the ancestral home of the Walronds. *E.S. Gosling collection*

Branscombe cottages, *c.*1894. These old cottages, which nestle snugly against the road, belong to the countryside and appear to have just grown there. The photographer who took this picture over 100 years ago successfully captured the timelessness of a village landscape. *E.S. Gosling collection*

General view of Branscombe village, *c.* 1890. Branscombe, a long and straggling village, had at this date a population of around 900. The valley in which it lies is still picturesque and beautifully wooded. In this picture you can see the sign for the Masons Arms quite plainly in the right foreground. *E.S. Gosling collection*

Looking towards Bank, Branscombe, 11 August 1877. The village streets at that time were not made up and were unlit. It will not do to imagine the Branscombe of nearly 130 years ago as a place of trim, clean cottages with flower gardens at the door and happy faces at the window. Some of it might have been like that, but the village also contained squalid hovels, and there is much less suffering and much more comfort in East Devon villages today. *E.S. Gosling collection*

The Masons Arms, Branscombe, 1961. Playing a vital part in our rural heritage, the Masons Arms in Branscombe still provides for most people the ideal image of a country pub. *E.S. Gosling collection*

Opposite below: Branscombe Beach. The derelict buildings at Branscombe mouth had been used to store the culm from South Wales to fuel the lime kilns on the cliffs, but by the time of this picture, they symbolised a vanished industry. *E.S. Gosling collection*

Axmouth village, 1899. Today's village bears little resemblance to the self-contained community of late Victorian days. Axmouth, like many of East Devon's villages, is now populated largely by former urbanites pursuing ephemera, aware of a lost dream but not of its reality. *E.S. Gosling collection*

The atmosphere of a Victorian Devon village is apparent in this 1885 photograph of Axmouth. The man with the horse and cart is standing outside the Harbour Inn, which in those days was a pub with sawdusted floors and solid wooden benches, where the farm and estate workers relaxed away from their employers. The children on the right were part of a village scene, now long gone, where the squire, Sanders Stephen Esq., still ruled and made sure that his tenants were in church on Sunday. *E.S. Gosling collection*

Axmouth village, 1953. There is an atmosphere of unhurried activity in this photograph of Axmouth taken half a century ago. East Devon was still an area of peaceful villages and sociable people, untouched by those with metropolitan attitudes who were to turn many of our villages into a form of countryside suburbia. *E.S. Gosling collection*

Axmouth village, 1952. *E.S. Gosling collection*

Across the River Axe from Seaton lies one of the oldest villages in England, Axmouth. Pictured here in 1958 the venerable church of St Michael. The church contains works of almost every period from Norman to Victorian. There are remains of the Norman church, *c.* 1150, and a narrow aisle which dates from the thirteenth century. *E.S. Gosling collection*

Stepps House, Axmouth, 1958. This long, old building, standing picturesquely on the right-hand side of the hill, was once a residence of importance. *E.S. Gosling collection*

Above: Axmouth village, 1958. When we look at these photographs of East Devon villages taken over forty-five years ago, we recognise their beauty and our loss. We can sense that something we once had has slipped from us and any gain is no compensation. *E.S. Gosling collection*

Right: Axmouth village, 1962. *E.S. Gosling collection*

This nostalgic view of the green in Colyton was taken in 1907. Since that date the landscape around Colyton has changed almost beyond recognition. The people of this small east Devon town thought that nothing from the outside world would ever be a threat to them or trouble the tranquil waters of this small stream, but the wars and troubles of the twentieth century were soon to intrude and change their lives for ever. *E.S. Gosling collection*

Opposite above: A delightful composition of Colyton's Chantry Bridge, *c.* 1890. *E.S. Gosling collection*

Opposite below: Gully Shoot corner, Colyford, 1890. *E.S. Gosling collection*

This pub was delicensed and is now a private house. *E.S. Gosling collection*

Musbury village, *c.* 1960. *E.S. Gosling collection*

Thatch at Whitford, 1961. There is nothing obtrusive about these old cottages; they do not dominate the landscape but look like a part of it. Generation after generation was born in them, lived their lives and passed away and, like good wine, their cottages have mellowed with age. *Ted Gosling collection*

Marlborough Cottage, Combpyne, 1937. This old thatched detached cottage with a wealth of oak belonged to the Rousdon Estate. At this time it was occupied by Mr R. Down, who worked for the estate. Marlborough Cottage was sold for £283 on Tuesday 14 September 1937 when over 140 lots of freehold property belonging to the Rousdon Estate were auctioned. *E.S. Gosling collection*

Branscombe Church, 1890. This parish church is dedicated to St Winifred, an obscure North Welsh saint who died around AD 650. For centuries, this old church has been the centre of village life; its walls are hallowed by the oft-repeated prayers of worshippers who mostly now rest beneath the grass of the churchyard. This photograph captures well the interior of one of the most atmospheric churches in Devon. *E.S. Gosling collection*

Seaton Junction, 1961. The opening in March 1868 of the branch line of the London and South Western Railway from Colyton Junction (as it was first called) marked a big step forward for the East Devon railway connection. Colyton Junction soon became Seaton Junction and for nearly 100 years this Seaton branch line served the community well until its closure in March 1966 following the Beeching Report. *E.S. Gosling collection*

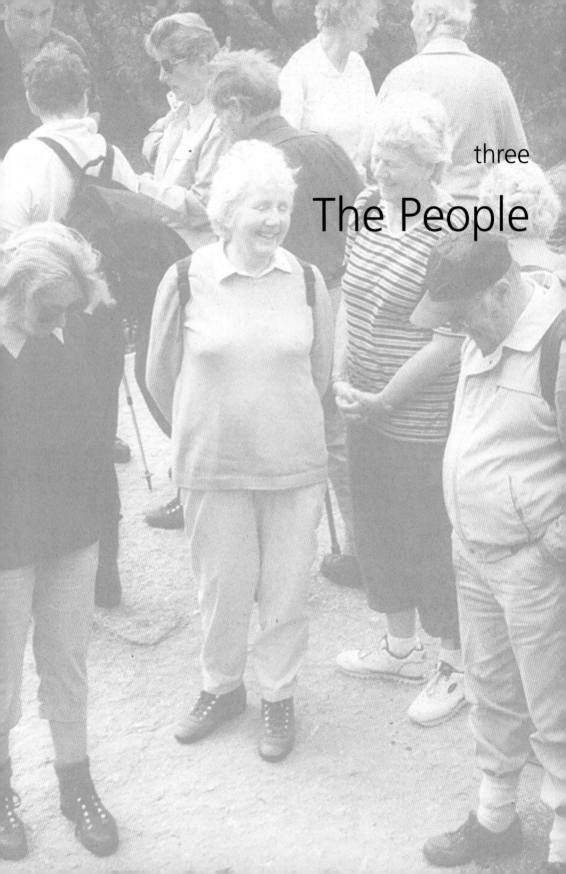

three

The People

Left: The Ugly Sisters at the Beer WI pantomime *Cinderella*, December 1932. *Seaton Museum*

Below: 'Age of Innocence'– Seaton girls pose on the West Walk during the summer of 1948 for this photograph. The lion was used by the beach photographer as a prop. *E.S. Gosling collection*

Above: Seaton firefighters pose for this 1960 picture. *E.S. Gosling collection*

Below: Red Cross presentation, *c.* 1974. *E.S. Gosling collection*

The first Boy Scout troop was formed in Seaton during April 1913, and Scouts were sworn in on 5 May 1913. Pictured here, resplendent with his many proficiency badges, we have young Archie Richards who became the local builder responsible for developments in The Orchard, The Close and Fortfield Terrace. *Seaton Museum*

Right: Charles Gosney, who was born in 1859, is pictured here during the early years of the twentieth century. Gosney became the first chemist in Seaton and he traded at his shop in Marine Parade until his death in 1935. One of his two daughters was Eileen Gosney who died in 1988 after devoting her life to researching the history of her native town. She was also a founder member of the Axe Valley Heritage Museum. *E.S. Gosling collection*

Below: Seaton Rugby Club, 1904. This picture was taken on the present-day football field. The large house in the background was called Hillymead; this property was demolished in the 1970s to make way for the Hillymead estate. Sport is always deeply engraved on popular memory and by 1904 conditions became favourable for sports like association football and rugby. Seaton had a highly successful rugby club and produced one player who was capped for the county and became first reserve for England. *Seaton Museum*

Looking sombre and serious, the pupils of Sir Walter Trevelyan's school, Seaton, pose for this class photograph in their playground, *c.* 1910. Junior teacher Miss Tozer can be seen standing on the left with a young Jenks White next to her. Jenks White retired from teaching in 1938 but came back to help teach in the school during the Second World War. Miss Tozer remained at the school until her retirement in 1949. Sadly she was killed by a car while crossing the road on Haldon Hill near Exeter. The headmaster at that time, Mr Oldridge, is standing on the left next to his wife and an unknown teacher. *Seaton Museum*

Left: Captain Heathcote, who lived in Colyford before the Second World War, is pictured here with his favourite cat in the garden of St Edmunds, his house. *E.S. Gosling collection*

Opposite above: The advent of Scouting was on 29 July 1907 when a party of twenty-two boys went to Brownsea Island under their leader, Robert Stephenson Smythe Baden-Powell. He felt that boys wanted an outdoor life and a chance to look after themselves away from their home environment. The idea of Scouting soon became world-famous, and the movement spread to every town throughout the UK. In this picture we have Cubs from the Beer Scouts in a photograph taken on 18 August 1931 at their camp at Weston. I am not sure why the young lady on the right was present but no doubt someone will tell me. *Seaton Museum*

Seaton Football Club veterans pose for this team picture at the local football field, *c.* 1949.
E.S. Gosling collection

Above: The Rev. Robert Sydney Robinson, vicar of St Gregory's parish church, pictured here second from the left, with other church members. Young Tom Clarke, the blacksmith's son, can be seen in the middle of the group. *Seaton Museum*

Left: George Henry Richards, who started the building business of G.C. Richards and Sons, at Parklands, Seaton in 1900. He was responsible for constructing many of Seaton's important buildings, including the Town Hall. George was an excellent builder and the houses he built are amongst the best in Seaton. *E.S. Gosling collection*

Right: John Gosling was born in Colyton in 1864 and left school at the age of ten to work on the building of Rousdon Mansion. He came to live in Seaton in 1908, becoming Head Gardener for Mr Edward Caselet Meade of Thornfield. A lifetime devout Plymouth Brother, he was a well-known figure in Seaton, acting as a judge at many local flower shows. John Gosling, who died in 1945, is seen here in the dress of a coachman in 1888 at a time when he worked at Halsdon House near Luppitt. *E.S. Gosling collection*

Left: Seaton and District Warship Week was held from 21 March to 28 March 1942. Following this week, a plaque was presented to HMS *Scarborough* to commemorate her adoption by the people of Seaton, Colyton, Beer and District during Warship Week. A future council allowed this plaque to be dumped but fortunately it was rediscovered, and here, in 1989, Ted Gosling, Curator of Seaton Museum, accepts the plaque to hang permanently in the Museum.
E.S. Gosling collection

Members of the England family who lived at the Landslip Cottage, *c.* 1913. From left to right: Beatrice, father Albert, Maud, mother Rose, Ethel, Elizabeth. *E.S. Gosling collection*

Firemen have performed an important role in the Seaton community during the past 110 years, and this photograph shows a part of their history. The picture is a unique and interesting photograph of the first horse-drawn fire engine in Seaton. It was taken in one of the old railway station buildings, *c.* 1895. The man standing with pride in front of the fire engine was Fire Chief Fred Abbott. *Seaton Museum*

Mr E. Bussell had a boot and shoe shop in Sidmouth Street, Seaton. This shop is now occupied by Bernard Pitts chemists. Bussell is seen here standing in his shop doorway, *c*. 1921. *Seaton Museum*

This photograph of holidaymakers walking towards the West Walk, Seaton, in 1934, successfully captures that era when the fashions in taste, thought, clothes and behaviour came to be thought of as 'Thirties'. *E.S. Gosling collection*

Opposite: Billy Freeman was what is often described as a 'character'. He spent most of his working life on Seaton beach selling fish and is pictured here in 1932 with a female admirer. *E.S. Gosling collection*

Right: Frank Barnicoat, 1953. Frank Barnicoat, who came to live in Seaton in 1946, was the uncle of local garage owner George Trevett. Frank was an accomplished photographer who had that rare gift of 'an eye for a picture'. He was a gentleman, much loved by all the locals. *E.S. Gosling collection*

Left: Stanley Pavey, who was born in Seaton, was a policeman based in Lynmouth, North Devon when on 15 August 1952 the small but popular resort was almost completely washed away in an horrific flood. Tragically, thirty-six people lost their lives in this disaster, which dominated the news around the world at the time. PC Pavey was on duty that night and courageously threw himself into the heart of the operation and worked tirelessly to save the lives of others. His bravery was rewarded by the Queen and he was presented with the British Empire Medal. Sadly, PC Pavey, who was later promoted to Sergeant, died a young man aged forty-eight, but the memory of his dedication and bravery will live on in his native town. *Joyce Grant*

The Golden Hind at Musbury was once known as the New Inn, and the landlady for many of the pre-war years was the popular Mrs Chard. Pictured outside the pub in 1930 are, from left to right: Jack Hannar, Eileen Salter (*née* Rockett) and her father, Ernest Rockett. *E.S. Gosling collection*

Miss Eileen Gosney is pictured here in 1936 walking past Mr Burnham's shop in Fore Street, Seaton. *Seaton Museum*

Seaton boys, 1946. Left to right: Derek Richards, Ted Gosling, Ralph Strang.
E.S. Gosling collection

Ferris and Prescott, the Seaton drapers, traded successfully in Queen Street for over forty years in premises occupied (at the time of this book) by the police station and the Age Concern centre. Mr Ferris retired in 1974, and is pictured here enjoying afternoon tea with his wife sitting on the left, with Miss Elizabeth Gosling on his right. *E.S. Gosling collection*

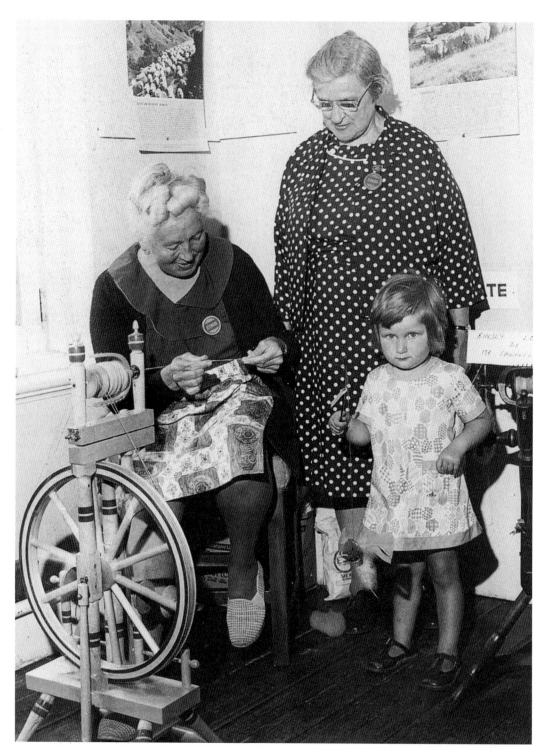

Mrs Thody pictured here at her spinning wheel at an exhibition held during the opening of St Clare's Adult Education Centre, July 1971. She is watched by the eldest and youngest exhibitors. *E.S. Gosling collection*

Roy and Rae Mills in the car park of the Long House in Harepath Road, holding young Rebecca Gosling, 1967. Mr & Mrs Mills took over the Long House restaurant in 1964, running it successfully until they retired in the early 1980s. It was then changed to a private house. They continued living there and are still residents at the time of this book. *E.S. Gosling collection*

'Where did you get that hat?' It was 1964 and these Seaton ladies had posed for this photograph after entering what appears to be a hat competition. *Seaton Museum – Tony Byrne-Jones*

Pictured here are Graham and Jessie Hilton in their Beer off-licence, *c.* 1978. At the time of this picture, they were providing an extra service to the village by enabling people to get their prescriptions dispensed because there was then no chemist in the village. People attending the doctors in Beer put their prescriptions in a bag in the surgery which was taken to the off-licence. A Seaton chemist came over for the prescriptions to dispense them, and then returned all the pills and lotions back to the off-licence daily. This certainly gives a new meaning to the old saying 'off to the pub for my medicine'! *Express and Echo*

Above: The collecting of matchbox labels is a hobby on a grand scale. There is even a name for it: phillumeny. There are thousands of different labels to be found with clubs, magazines and meetings supporting the hobby. Well-known Seaton character Bob Hayes was a keen phillumenist and is pictured here *c.* 1978 displaying a section of his huge collection.
E.S. Gosling collection

Left: The popular Klaus Peters and his wife Shirley, together with their Great Dane, pose in this picture at the rear of their restaurant Copperfields, *c.* 1975.

Above: Violet Webster, pictured in 1989. Mrs Webster's father, Herbert Good, owned the Cliff House Hotel on Castle Hill. The Goods were one of the oldest Seaton families and Mrs Webster possessed an unrivalled knowledge of her native town. *Seaton Museum*

Left Miss Elizabeth Gosling is seen standing on the right of this photograph with two friends from Chard during September 1984. Known to all people as Aunt Ciss, she was much loved for her wonderful sense of humour. She delighted in taking out trays of tea to any builder or road repairer who was working outside her house in Sidmouth Street. *E.S. Gosling collection*

Above: John Scott and Gladys Gray are seen here with the later medieval window tracery, originally in Colyton Church and now in Beer Quarry Caves underground museum. *Express and Echo*

Right: A few days before the advent of the new millennium, the three surviving members of the original Seaton Museum Committee stood in the doorway of Seaton Town Hall for this founders' photograph. Left to right: Mr Roy Chapple, Chairman, Mrs Edna Everitt, Friends of the Museum Secretary, and Ted Gosling, Curator and Secretary. At the time of this picture they had all served in their respective offices for fourteen years. *E.S. Gosling collection*

Above: Members of the Axe Valley Runners who took part in the Bridgwater half-marathon. Left to right: Steve Boyes, Steve Atkins, John Masson, Harry Moore, with Steve White kneeling in front of the group. *H. Moore*

Right: Seaton's marathon man, Harry Moore, is seen here taking part in the Great West Run, 5 May 1996. Harry started running competitively in 1984 when he took part in the Torvill and Dean Olympic Appeal. By the end of April 2003 he had completed 745 runs including 130 half-marathons. This achievement earned him a place in the Devon athletic record books, and he just missed out being in the Guinness Book of Records. *H. Moore*

Frogs spawn in March and the female will shed up to 3,000 eggs for the male to fertilise. At the end of May the tadpoles hatch but very few survive to adulthood. We all know that children love to collect a few tadpoles to keep in jam jars but here, on 4 July 2002, members of the AVHA on a Dartmoor walk with tour guide Tony Burgess (seen on the far right), stop near Haytor to inspect with fascination a Dartmoor pool teeming with tadpoles. *Seaton Museum*

Training lecture in the dugout for Seaton Town football players, 1973. *E.S. Gosling collection*

Above: Seaton's youth theatre group, STARS, was formed by Lynne Derrick in 1999. Their first production, *A Musical Centenary*, was staged in the July of that year at the Methodist Church in Valley View. In November 1999 the group performed the Dickens classic, *A Christmas Carol*, at Seaton Town Hall under the direction of Anne Giles. April 2000 saw a stunning performance of *The Wizard of Oz* followed in November with *Toad of Toad Hall*. Other productions since then have included *Alice in Wonderland*, *The Car* and *The Dracula Spectacular Show*. All of the cast are aged between ten and sixteen years old and much credit must go to the children and the dedication of Lynne Derrick and her team of willing helpers. Here is the cast of STARS' first production, *A Musical Centenary*, which was staged at the Methodist Church Hall in July 1999. *Colin Bowerman*

Opposite above: The cast of *The Wizard of Oz* pictured in Windsor Gardens in April 2000. *Colin Bowerman*

Opposite below: Alice – The Musical was STARS' seventh production staged at Seaton Town Hall. November 2001 *STARS*

Left: Ron Durrans was born in 1920 in the town of Guisborough in the Cleveland district of the old North Riding of Yorkshire. The depression of the 1930s hit that part of the country and Ron, aged sixteen, left his family home at Marske-by-Sea on 3 March 1937 to come for work in Seaton as part of the Juvenile Transference scheme. When he arrived at Seaton station, he was escorted to his lodgings at 9 Sidmouth Street, near the site of the old post office and the present sorting office. The family who lived there were a Mr & Mrs G. Chedzoy and their thirteen-year-old daughter, Linda. The house was lit by gas, and water was obtained from a pump in the yard. Coming from a modern semi-detached house with all mod cons, it was like a step back in time for him. After a short time the Chedzoys and their lodgers relocated to 14 Summerland Place. Ron Durrans started work the next day for K.F. Mottram, the local builder, and stayed in Seaton until 1938. Ron Durrans is pictured here, aged seventeen, on West Cliff.

Right: Jim McGuirk, another lodger, is pictured with Mr G. Chedzoy at 14 Summerland Place. Mr Chedzoy was then seventy-three years old and had, in his younger days, been a patient of W.G. Grace, the cricketer. *Seaton Museum*

Seventeen-year-old Dick Bromley, another boy from Sunderland on the Juvenile Transference Scheme, is seen here on the left with Sam Ayres of Axmouth in 1937. *Seaton Museum*

One of the houses built by K.F. Mottram, *c.* 1936, on New Beer Road. The purchase price at that time was £2,500. *Seaton Museum*

Seaton Juniors Rugby Team, 1912. Before the First World War, rugby football was almost a religion in the town and here, on the football field, on a typical English December day long ago, the juniors posed for this pre-match photograph. Little did they know then that within three years the innocence of their youth would disappear in the hell of such places as Vimy Ridge, Ypres, Somme, Kut and Gallipoli. However, on this day, that was not only in the future but beyond their comprehension.
E.S. Gosling collection

George Trevett, the well-known Seaton garage owner, is pictured here in 1937 setting off for a motorcycle trial. *Seaton Museum*

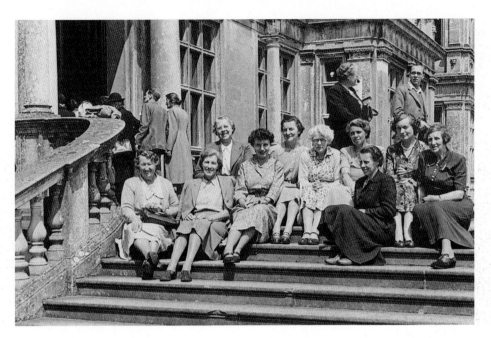

Above: Seaton WI ladies pose on the steps of Longleat House for this souvenir picture of their visit in 1953. *Seaton Museum*

Below: Ladies of the Seaton congregational church in Cross Street at a tea party in 1975. *Tony Byrne-Jones*

Seaton cricket, *c.* 1903. Viewed across a century of war and economic crisis, the England of Edward VII appears to have been a place of peace and prosperity, and this photograph captures the atmosphere of that brief Indian summer. This picture came from Gwendoline Marsh's album, and we see her sitting in front on the right. Gwendoline was a member of a solid, established professional family. Her father was a solicitor in Yeovil and they came to Seaton every year for a month's holiday. Seaton then, as now, had a first-rate cricket ground where, during the summer, travelling and local teams competed with the hosts. Here, the Marsh family and friends pose for this charming photograph, taken during the tea break. *E.S. Gosling collection*

Right: Mr Ben Trevett, the Seaton garage owner, was photographed taking his daughter to Axmouth church for her wedding during the summer months of 1919. *Seaton Museum*

Below: Colyton St John Ambulance Brigade cadets, *c.* 1950. *E.S. Gosling collection*

Jim Knight moved to Seaton in 1982. Since then he has spent twelve years as a town councillor, holding various portfolios. He has been mayor twice and was chairman of Cliff Field Gardens and Seaton in Bloom. In May 1999 he was elected as a district councillor.

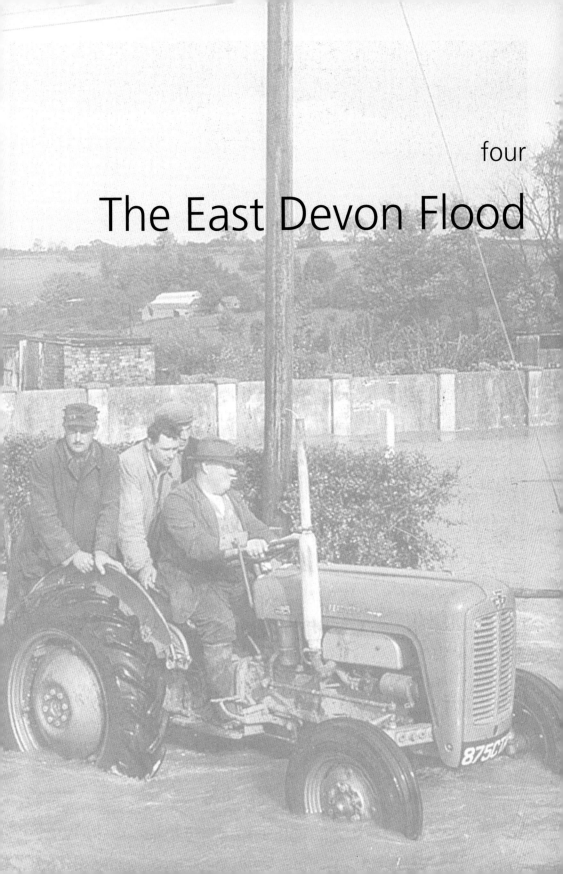

four

The East Devon Flood

The worst disaster in living memory to hit East Devon came at about 3 o'clock in the morning of 1 October 1960, when three inches of rain cascaded down and within minutes, the centuries-old village of Axmouth, lying right on the River Axe, the ancient town of Colyton, bordered by the River Coly, and the tiny village of Whitford were swimming in water. Seaton Police Sergeant Donald Cowling received an SOS call at 3.30 a.m., and together with PC George Rodd, he drove to Axmouth to find the main road had disappeared underwater. More than forty houses in the village took the full brunt of the water, leaving them after the flood with inches of black slimy mud covering the floors and furniture. Local photographer Tony Byrne-Jones took these remarkable and unique pictures of the flood featured in this chapter. At Colyton the flooded river swamped low-lying houses and torrents of water came down from the hills, which ripped up roads and turned the bottom of the town into a lake. These two photographs show the inundated area at Colyton after the Coly burst its banks.

This widespread flooding caused many problems in Colyton, and the extent of the flooding near Road Green can be seen in these two photographs, although the local farmer in his tractor seems to be taking it all in his stride.

Above: An Express Dairy lorry on the road from Road Green, Colyton.

Below: In Axmouth the damage to the roads was almost unbelievable. Where the torrent had crossed a road there was usually a mass of broken tarmac; where it had run down a road, the tarmac had just disappeared. In the picture you can see the damage at the bottom of Stepps Lane.

Above: Note the state of the road near Coombe Orchard.

Below: This was the scene on the main road at Axmouth where houses were flooded and tons of stones washed into the road.

Cleaning up after the flood was an arduous and unpleasant job, and many people lost virtually all their downstairs belongings. Here we have local residents in Axmouth baling out water from their cottages. Unfortunately these thatched cottages were demolished at a much later date and replaced with a modern building.

Opposite above: For the second time in four days, 7.14 inches of rain fell at Axmouth, and on the fateful morning, 3.87 inches fell, leaving scenes like this. Extremely heavy rain fell in the catchment area of the small stream which runs down the centre of the village. The force of the water carried trees and boulders, which built up a dam. When the dam broke, a tidal wave swept through the village.

Opposite below: Nobody who has not seen the aftermath of a flood can ever imagine the devastation. Here the flood-hit residents in Axmouth are trying to cope by putting out precious belongings and furniture to dry.

Houses in this area of Axmouth were flooded to a depth of five feet and this householder appears to be wondering where to start. After the flood, parties of boys from Axmouth and Seaton went round asking people if they could help clear up the mess.

High winds and heavy rain caused damage to the Spot On refreshment hut on the East Walk in 1962. You can see by this photograph that teas and sandwiches were not on the menu that day.

There is little one can do against nature in full spate. In Seaton it was a case of too much water pouring into the Harbour Road area and the adjoining marshes which are, after all, just a few feet above normal sea level; a lesson to be learnt here for any proposed development on this flood plain. In the top picture we have an exterior view of Trevett's garage in Harbour Road, and in the lower one, the scene inside showing the flooded cars.

A young Roger Webber, seen in the middle, surveys the damage to the Chine in Seaton.

Heavy rain contributed to this cliff fall onto the West Walk, Seaton in 1960. *Tony Byrne-Jones*

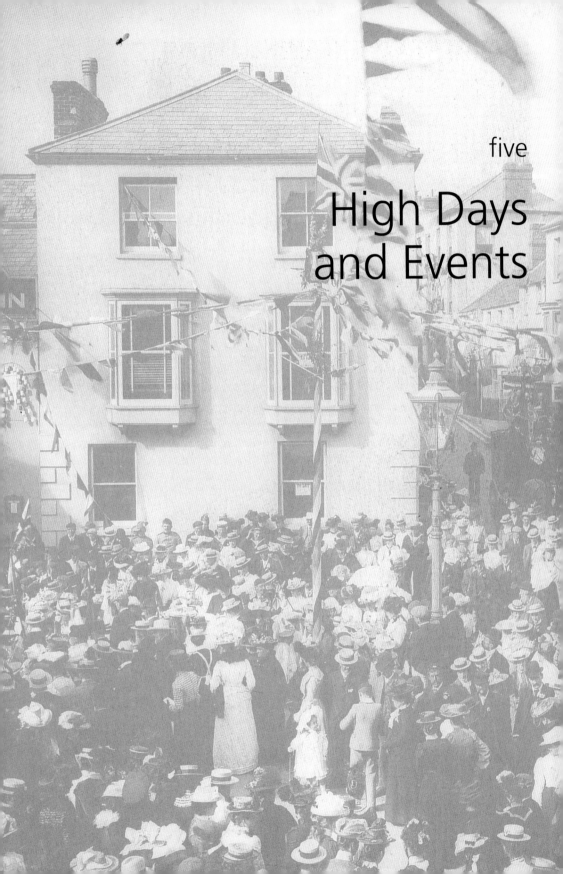

five

High Days
and Events

Above: Queen Victoria's Diamond Jubilee celebrations, Beer 1897. The possibilities of a great celebration in 1897 were first discussed after the Golden Jubilee of 1887, although it was not until 1896 that public interest in the event was thoroughly aroused. Every town and village formed a committee to arrange activities for the great day and everywhere the streets were lavishly decorated. Here, the people of Seaton gather in the Square to take part in the celebrations. It would be safe to say that every town and village in Great Britain had its own procession, its own feast for the poor, its sports or its firework display. Here in Seaton, on that far-off Jubilee Day of 22 June 1897, following a stormy night, the sun appeared to give meaning to the expression 'Queen's Weather'. It was the sixtieth anniversary of the reign of the best-loved of all Britain's sovereigns, and the people standing here in the Square in the mid-morning sunlight knew that they were a part of the greatest empire the world had ever known. *E.S. Gosling collection*

Opposite above: Pictured here are the triumphant arches that spanned Fore Street in Beer for Queen Victoria's Diamond Jubilee celebrations in 1897. Standing in the doorway of their home, No.1 Gravel Cottage, are Lizzie and Bob Boles with family members. *E.S. Gosling collection*

Opposite below: The Seaton Town Hall was built by local builder Mr G. Richards, and the opening ceremony took place on 27 July 1904. The Town Hall soon became the social centre of Seaton and featured, among other attractions, roller skating. Unfortunately, this had to cease owing to the damage incurred to the floor. The Edwardians loved to dress up and even in a small town like Seaton, the locals had their evenings filled with diversity and interest. This picture was taken in Seaton Town Hall during the winter of 1905, and the people in this photograph were at a roller skating fancy dress party. Note the roller skates worn by the people in the foreground. The only person I can recognise is the lady in white sitting in the second row in the middle, the wife of W.H. Head Esq. from the Wessiters. *E.S. Gosling collection*

During the clear, cloudless, blue, hot days of August 1913 the Seaton Scouts spent many nights under canvas in the old vicarage field. In this picture, Scouts are busy with various activities, while the elm trees in the background provide a leafy shade from the midday sun. *E.S. Gosling collection*

Opposite above: False moustaches appeared to be the order of the day in this picture, taken at the Wessiters in 1901. They were members of the Seaton Rugby Club who had entered a tableau for that year's Carnival. The entry was a skit on Evans' George Inn. *E.S. Gosling collection*

Opposite below: Seaton church parade, *c.* 1925. A fine picture with considerable visual interest, showing the Rev. R.G. Robinson, vicar of Seaton, heading the parade in his car. He is followed by the town band, the Boy Scouts and members of his Sunday School. The man with the white coat on the right of the picture was Mr Burnside, the dentist who had his surgery in Seafield Terrace. Seafield on the left was still undeveloped, although properties were beginning to be built on the top end of Castle Hill. *E.S. Gosling collection*

Ted Gosling, aged four years old, is sitting in the middle of this group of formidable ladies. They were members of the Women's Meeting from Seaton Gospel Hall. His grandmother and his Aunt Ciss can be seen in the back row, and they were all enjoying a day's coach outing to Dartmoor. *E.S. Gosling collection*

Seaton Gospel Hall members on a day's trip to the Cheddar Caves, *c.* 1927. The excitement of a day out in a charabanc is reflected in their faces. Few people had cars in those days and destinations like the Cheddar Caves were inaccessible to most. *E.S. Gosling collection*

Above: Colyton Carnival float by F.J. Baker and Co., *c.* 1952. The ladies on the float are, from left to right, Mrs Facey, Kit Pilgrim and Nina Brewer. *Seaton Museum*

Below: Because Seaton Town Hall was still out of commission following the disastrous fire of 1945, carnival events in 1952 were held in a marquee on the Seaton cricket field. Mary Gooding, sitting in the chair, was the Carnival Queen that year, and her attendants were Marion Powling on the left and Barbara Newton on the right. The crowning ceremony was performed by Mrs Shand, seen on the left of this photograph. *E.S. Gosling collection*

The distinguished author, playwright and critic, Mr St John Ervine, came to live in Seaton during the 1930s in the house 'Honey Ditches' which was built for him on Seaton Down. He is pictured here at an unknown function which took place in Seaton during the early 1950s. Ervine is standing on the left with his wife, Leonora, beside him. Frank Norcombe, who was then chairman of Seaton Town Council, is seen in the middle of the group with Mrs Paddy Norcombe on his left. *Seaton Museum*

Many familiar faces in this 1950s photograph, taken in the Seaton congregational church on Cross Street, at a Christmas party for OAPs. Not sure why they are holding up the cards but they could be some form of Christmas present. *E.S. Gosling collection*

Above: The opening ceremony of the Mariners Hall, Beer, Saturday 13 September 1958. Arthur Edward Good gave the Mariners Hall to the village of Beer with the thought that it would serve as a memorial to the considerable number of master marines that the village had produced, as well as to those inhabitants who had made 'the calling of the sea' their livelihood. Arthur Good was a Master Mariner, one of over 140 men from Beer who achieved this rank. Pictured here outside the Mariners Hall following the ceremony are, left to right, the Rev. W.H. Dormer, vicar of Beer, Percy Westlake MM, chairman of Beer Parish Council, Arthur Edward Good MM, Mrs Good and Derek Oliver Good, chairman of the Management Committee. *Express and Echo*

Right: Souvenir programme of events in Axmouth to celebrate the Silver Jubilee of Queen Elizabeth II. *E.S. Gosling collection*

Souvenir Programme
of Events to Celebrate the

Silver Jubilee

of Her Most Gracious Majesty
Queen Elizabeth II

——— in Axmouth ———

on Tuesday June 7th 1977 at 2.15 p.m.
at Axe Farm Camping Site

(By kind permission of Mr K. Webber)

COMMITTEE: *Chairman* - Mrs B. Martin, *Secretary* - Mrs M. Hancock, *Treasurer* - Mrs B. Bater
Members - Mrs D. Hart, Miss N. Sweetland, Mrs P. Middleton, Mrs E. Gush, Mrs B. Down,
Mrs R. Tidball, Miss M. Newberry, Miss M. L. Broom

Sir Arthur Seymour Sullivan, the English musical composer, collaborated with Sir William Schwenck Gilbert to produce the light comic operas they are so famous for. The Axe Vale Amateur Operatic Society have delighted local audiences with performances of Gilbert and Sullivan's works for many years and here, in the top picture, we have the cast of *Iolanthe* in a 1957 production. If you did not know, Iolanthe was a fairy princess who fell in love with a mortal and was banished to live with the frogs. The bottom picture shows the society thirty-one years on with a new production of *Iolanthe* in April 1988. Mary Byrne-Jones, who took part in both productions, can be seen in the top picture, front left, and in the bottom picture, third lady from the left in the second row up. *Seaton Museum*

SEATON AND DISTRICT CHORAL SOCIETY.

President:—SIR WALTER J. TREVELYAN, BART.

GRAND Concert

TUESDAY, MARCH 3RD, 1925.

In the TOWN HALL, SEATON.

Performance by Members of the Society, of **MENDELSSOHN'S**

HYMN of PRAISE

Soloists:—MISS EYRE POWELL, Soprano ;
MR. A. WARD KENNEDY, Tenor
(Exeter Cathedral.)

Orchestra : Hon. Conductor — **MR. W. C. WALTON.**
Hon. Accompanist — **MISS N. GOULD.**

Violinist : MISS PHYLLIS SMITH, of Exeter.

Part Songs by Members of the Society.

Doors open, 7 p.m. Commence 7.30.

PRICES , including Tax **3/6** RESERVED AND NUMBERED ; **2/4** ; AND A LIMITED NUMBER AT **1/3.**
Reserved unnumbered · unreserved

Seats may be booked at MISS ABBOTT'S, THE SQUARE, SEATON.

MISS M. GUNN
DR. A. H. J. SMART } Hon. Secs.

W. Smith's Library, Printers, Seaton   And at Colyton.

Seaton and District Choral Society, Grand Concert programme, Tuesday 3 March 1925.
E.S. Gosling collection

Mr Snell, the secretary of the Seaton Camera Club, stands beside the exhibition of photographs which the club organised for the opening ceremony of St Clare's Adult Education centre in July 1971. *E.S. Gosling collection*

A frustrating feature of the work of a museum curator responsible for the collection of old photographs is the large number which bear neither date nor subject's name. Although I can recognise many familiar faces in this 1970s photograph, any additional information would be welcome. *E.S. Gosling collection*

Geoffrey Ellerton, chairman of the Seaton District Hospital League of Friends, is pictured here standing on the left with Dr Bob Jones on the right, ready to cut the first turf for the new hospital in 1986. *Seaton Museum*

The Seaton Hospital League of Friends held a coffee morning at Netherhayes in 1989, in aid of hospital funds. Mary Wood, the organiser, is seen here with helpers, sitting at the front table. *Seaton Museum*

Above: Ted Gosling was accompanied by Sandra Moore from Sidmouth when he attended the opening of the new National Motor Museum at Beaulieu in 1958. He is pictured here at Beaulieu in his 1924 vintage Bullnose Morris. This car was bought for £10 in an unrestored condition and complete restoration took Ted a year to complete. *E.S. Gosling collection*

Right: Members of the Axe Valley Heritage Association give a smile for the man with the camera at their Christmas Dinner, which in 1999 was held at the Wheelwright in Colyford. *Seaton Museum*

Just over 2,000 years ago a new hope entered the world with the birth of Jesus and Christianity survived against all odds to reach the twentieth century, the atomic age and the new millennium. This was welcomed by a firework party that lit up the whole world, and across Britain a chain of beacons symbolically linked the country. Throughout East Devon the night sky was transformed by starbursts of pink, silver and gold as rockets were launched with spectacular effect and at the stroke of midnight from Big Ben, thousands of people danced, sang and hugged each other. In the top picture, Axe Valley Heritage members assemble outside Seaton Town Hall to have this millennium photograph taken by local photographer Chris Byrne-Jones. In the bottom picture, local children line up for face painting at a millennium party in the town hall. *Seaton Museum*

Before the present waterside road was built from Seaton to Axmouth in 1925, flooding was a common occurrence. This picture, taken in 1924, shows construction work on the new road.
E.S. Gosling collection

It was on 22 March 1927 that the tender of Messrs N. Pratt & Son to build the new Colyton Grammar School was accepted. It was to be the first purpose-built secondary school of the century in Devon and it opened on 15 January 1929. In this photograph some of the building workforce had assembled for a picture, *c.* 1928. *E.S. Gosling collection*

There are eight bells in the towers of St Gregory's church, two of which were added as a memorial to the twenty-four men of Seaton who fell in the First World War. One of these bells was entirely subscribed for by the women of the parish. A further two were added in 1948 in memory of those who fell in the Second World War. This photograph was taken when the two First World War bells were hung, *c.* 1921. *E.S. Gosling collection*

Members from the Women's Meeting, Seaton Gospel Hall, had a narrow escape when, on a coach outing, the vehicle left the road and slid into a ditch. Apart from the shock, no-one was hurt and here we have some of the party discussing the event, *c.* 1965. *E.S. Gosling collection*

Previous page below: Boer War Peace Day, Seaton Square, May 1902. The Boer War cost Britain £270 million and by forcing the British to use 400,000 troops against the outnumbered Boers, it revealed to the rest of Europe the weaknesses of British military power. The Boer War ended in May 1902 and was the climax of late Victorian imperialism. In Seaton the Peace Day was celebrated with much joy; many local young men were serving in the Army and Sir Redvers Buller, who was sent to South Africa in 1899 as Chief Commander, came from Crediton and was immensely popular in Devon.
E.S. Gosling collection

There was great excitement in Beer in 1926 when a De Havilland aeroplane crash-landed on Beer Common. Clapp's Transport were given the job to return the plane to the De Havilland works and in this picture you can see the wings with a part of the tailplane sticking out of the rear of the lorry. The people in the picture are, from left to right: Mr Tidcombe, Stanley Oborn, local garage owner Mr W.L. Oborn, Bill Keate, who drove the lorry, and Harry Clapp. *E.S. Gosling collection*

Opening of the West Walk, 1925. The old West Walk was washed away during a storm in 1915 and was replaced by the present walk in 1924. The coping stone was laid by the chairman of Seaton Urban District Council, Mr C.C. Gould, in 1924 and in this picture we have the official opening performed by Morrison Bell, the local MP, in 1925. *E.S. Gosling collection*

East Devon was almost cut off from the outside world when a blizzard hit the area over a weekend in mid-February 1978. Outlying farms and cottages were isolated for almost a week and the snow drifted so high, it was possible to walk over the tops of hedges. A strange, uncanny silence filled the towns of Seaton and Colyton due to the complete absence of traffic. The residents lived for a few days in a snow-muffled world, and the main road to Exeter was blocked for five days. In the top picture a man with a broom makes a futile effort to brush back the snow in the centre of Colyton, and in the bottom picture, there is another view of Colyton in Queens Square. *Seaton Museum*

Above: Dancing around the village maypole was once a pagan fertility custom. At one time it was the custom for a tree to be cut down and brought in from the woods in the early morning of May Day. But here, in 1995, the girls with their serious-looking partners prepare to dance around the maypole in Colyton Square to commemorate the 50th anniversary of VE Day. *John Lavers*

Right: Ted Gosling is pictured here presenting a cup to Miss Seaton, the 1993 Seaton Carnival Queen, after the crowning ceremony. Carnival chairman Roger Woolland can be seen on the right. *E.S. Gosling collection*

Members of Seaton Youth Club worked hard to create a set of incredible colourful mosaics which were unveiled on Saturday 23 March 1997 outside the Marshlands Day Centre for the elderly in Marsh Road. The eight 8ft x 5ft mosaics made from bathroom tiles and broken crockery each depicted scenes from Seaton's history in a myriad of colours. The panels were unveiled by the following dignitaries seen here:

Panel 1	The Romans	Mrs Dearden-Potter, Seaton Town Council
Panel 2	The Vikings	Mr T Gosling, Local Historian
Panel 3	The Smugglers	Julie Clark & Bridget Crump, East Devon
Panel 4	Beer Quarry Caves	Kurt Parry, Westcountry Television
Panel 5	The Railways	Alan Cotton, EDAC Board
Panel 6	The Victorians	Manager & Residents, Marshlands Day Centre
Panel 7	The Tramways	Sarah Randal Johnson, Amenities Committee, EDDC
Panel 8	The New Youth Club	Representatives of Trustees and members of Seaton Youth Centre

Chris Byrne-Jones

Above: The Regal Cinema, Seaton. This cinema, which opened in 1938 and stood on the site of the present Windsor Gardens, provided family entertainment for the town until its closure in 1972. The closure and subsequent demolition of the Regal Cinema caused much feeling in the town and in this picture we have the demolition work well in hand. *E.S. Gosling collection*

Below: Members of the Axe Valley Heritage Association browse around Blackbury Castle when the association paid a visit to the site in 1987. *E.S. Gosling collection*

Left: Trevett's breakdown lorry pictured in 1957 outside Trevett's filling station on Harbour Road, the site now occupied by the Rainbow complex. *E.S. Gosling collection*

Below: Dick Tregaskis in the cab of the station wagon, *c.* 1937. Tregaskis operated a transport company and was an agent for the Southern Railway. *Seaton Museum*

SCHOOL FOR YOUNG GENTLEMEN,

THE OLD SCHOOL-ROOM,

(NEAR SEATON CHURCH.)

MR. WILLIAMS, holding a high class Certificate from the Government; formerly Head Master of the Royal Free Schools, Windsor; and some time Inspector of Government Schools in the West Indies, respectfully announces to the Inhabitants of Seaton, Beer, and the neighbourhood, that he proposes to establish a School for a select number of Young Gentlemen at the Old School Room, near Seaton Church, and to commence duties on MONDAY, NOVEMBER,

MR. WILLIAMS has had many years' experience in educational work, and will devote unremitting attention to the moral and intellectual training of the pupils committed to his care.

THE SCHOOL COURSE will include all the usual subjects of a sound English education—

    Reading, Writing, and Arithmetic.
    English Grammar, Composition, and Literature.
    History, especially of our own country.
    Geography, Natural Science, etc.

THE SCHOOL FEES will be **One Guinea per Quarter**.

(They will be charged according to that rate from the date of entrance to Christmas next.)

MR. WILLIAMS begs to intimate that his daughters the MISSES WILLIAMS have established **a School for Young Ladies** at Elm Grove Colyton; the prospectus of which can be obtained by post, or by application at his School Room in Seaton.

PIANOFORTE LESSONS.

MISS WILLIAMS gives instruction at Elm Grove, Colyton, to Young Ladies desiring pianoforte lessons, on a first class Broadwood instrument, and proposes to attend music pupils at their homes in Seaton.

TERMS ON APPLICATION.

ELM GROVE, COLYTON,
    27th October, 1879.

1879 advertisement for a school for young gentlemen in the old school room near Seaton Church. *Seaton Museum*

Above: A group of Seatonians stop at Dartmeet in this splendid Lancia charabanc, *c.* 1924. *E.S. Gosling collection*

Left: Rocket and sea rescue practice in Beer, *c.* 1928. *E.S. Gosling collection*

Meet of the Axe Vale Harriers, *c.* 1926. *E.S. Gosling collection*

Seaton choir outing, *c.* 1930. In the centre is the vicar, Rev. Robinson. Front row, left to right: Mr D Taylor, Mr Good, Mr B. Gillard, Mr Taylor. Others include Mr and Mrs Northcott, Mr and Mrs H. Clapp, Mr and Mrs Hoskins, Mr C.C. Gould and Mrs D. Newton. *E.S. Gosling collection*

Members of the Axe Valley Heritage Association enjoy a celebration lunch at The Kettle, held to celebrate chairman Roy Chapple's seventieth birthday. *E.S. Gosling collection*

six

In Times of War

Above: For many years the Seaton Fire Station was on the site now occupied by Local Plus supermarket. During their time at this station, members of the fire service played an important part in the community with help for everything from chimney fires to car accidents, from major fires to floods, and the much praised help during the Exeter Blitz. This is a group photograph taken during the Second World War. *E.S. Gosling collection*

Below: The skilful, dedicated men and women of the National Fire Service during the Second World War must never be forgotten. In this picture we have men from the Seaton National Fire Service, who played a heroic part in the defence of Exeter and Plymouth during enemy bombing. They were pictured standing outside the local fire station, *c.* 1944. The man kneeling beside the pump on the right was the much respected local, Bill Keate. *Seaton Museum*

These two unique photographs show all that was left of the house called Seafield, which stood in the present Jubilee Gardens, following an air raid during the Second World War. During the period from August 1940 to 1943, East Devon was subjected to many air raids and on 26 October 1942, a German hit-and-run raider dropped bombs on Seaton. Seafield, which stood at the corner of Seahill and Castle Hill, was hit and demolished, resulting in the death of the Cartwright family who were having lunch at the time. This picture, taken the following day shows the remains of the house, in the photograph below, taken at the same time, you can see the bomb crater and the walls of Kingsland, the house next door to Seafield. *Seaton Museum*

The day before Britain entered the First World War was the August Bank Holiday Monday, and on that day – a day of unclouded sunshine – hundreds of people lined the road from Beer to Seaton station to see the Army and Navy Reservists leave by special trains. Thanks to a well-prepared operation called the War Book, everyone knew what to do. A Reservist would have received that day a telegram with only one word – 'Mobilise' – and with this they could obtain a rail warrant to their destination. In the top picture you can see the Beer Naval Reservists marching up Long Hill surrounded by cheering crowds. In the bottom picture we have them again, well on the road to Seaton. *E.S. Gosling collection*

Right and below: At the outbreak of the
Second World War, new factories for the
munitions drive were soon planned, and
Sydney Pritchard and his brother William
won a contract to produce shell fuses and
aircraft components. Their factory in
Holloway, North London, was moved to
the garage in Branscombe Square and had a
workforce of 114 men and women working
day and night in twelve-hour shifts. In the
top picture, *c.* 1943, the factory van driver,
Jim White, is seen loading up shell fuses for
delivery to Seaton Station. In the bottom
picture, taken at the same time, is an
interior picture of the factory. *E.S. Gosling
collection*

Left: Wartime bus conductresses Kitty Andrews, Dorothy ? and Peg Seager photographed with bus driver Giles White from Beer at the Station Road bus depot, Seaton, 1942. During the Second World War the courage, action and endurance of Britain's women was evident in all areas and walks of life – in the Army, the Navy and the Air Force, as Land Army Girls, at fire stations and in factories. *E.S. Gosling collection*

Colyton Home Guard, *c.* 1943. The plan of raising Local Defence Volunteers in 1940 met with an immediate response from all over the country. The name was soon changed to the Home Guard, although they were affectionately known as 'Dad's Army'. These men from Colyton played an important part in the Second World War, and after their final muster in 1945, much appreciation was felt by all for the voluntary work they had done during the difficult days of war. *E.S. Gosling collection*

seven

The Seaside

A fine picture of sailing luggers hauled up, stern first, on Beer Beach, *c.* 1890. Some of these were used for carrying stone to West Bay and Exmouth. *E.S. Gosling collection*

Beer Beach, 1929. Photographs admirably convey scenes of a long-past time and there is a magic in this picture, taken on Beer beach, which brings a lost landscape to life with its full range of evocations and associations. *E.S. Gosling collection*

During the first week of October 1896, the South of England was swept by a succession of heavy gales which did a great deal of damage on land and wrought much havoc on the coast. It was during those gales that the *Berar*, a three-masted Italian barque, was on her way from Finland to Spain laden with about 1,200 tons of planks and, in tacking from the Casquets off the coast of France to Start Point in the face of strong westerly gales, the captain unsuccessfully attempted to make for Portland. He lost his bearings, and the force of the wind and waves drove her broadside onto the rocks about 200 yards on the Seaton side of the Rousdon boundary. The jagged rocks soon tore her plates asunder and she quickly filled with water. The crew, consisting of Captain Bertolotto, thirteen men and two boys, scrambled over the sides and reached dry land in safety. In the top picture is the *Berar* on the rocks and the bottom picture shows the vessel two days later, after further rough seas had caused her to break in two. *E.S. Gosling collection*

Cliffside potato fields, Branscombe, *c.* 1910. The Branscombe cliffs sheltered these plots from the cold winds, enabling the cliff farmers to grow the earliest potatoes in the country. *E.S. Gosling collectio*

Beach huts and deckchairs were the order of the day in this 1928 photograph of Seaton beach, looking towards White Cliff. *E.S. Gosling collection*

The clubhouse of Axe Cliff Golf Club, c. 1925. At the time of this photograph, the President was Miss Sanders Stephens and the Hon. Secretary Mr F. Gogill. The course of eighteen holes commanded magnificent views for many miles inland, and from Portland Bill to the Start Point on the seaward side. *E.S. Gosling collection*

A delightful picture of a little girl carrying a bucket and spade, walking along the old East walk wall adjoining Seaton beach, c. 1919. Note the splendid Victorian shelter in the background which then stood on The Burrow. *E.S. Gosling collection*

As part of a scheme to prevent flooding from the sea, a new £600,000 sea wall and promenade was built at Seaton by South-West Water. In the top picture, taken on 12 January 1980, you can see the old sea wall demolished. In the bottom picture, taken on 30 September 1980, with the sea wall near completion, workmen are drilling holes to attach the gate hinges to the wall. *Seaton Museum*

Lionel and Garnet Miller, two Beer fishermen, standing beside a capstan on Beer Beach, 1938. *E.S. Gosling collection*

A surprise visit to Seaton beach by this hovercraft in 1966 astonished visitors and residents alike. *Seaton Museum*

Although Brixham held its position as the leading fishing port in the country until recent times, an old saying in Beer went 'Beer made Brixham and Brixham made the North Sea'. This was quite true, as the first fishermen to trawl from Brixham were men of Beer in their small boats. The best weather for trawling was a stiff breeze of not less than force 6, but this made the old Beer luggers weatherbound on the beach because Beer did not have a harbour. As a result Brixham, with its harbour, became the trawling centre. Despite this, Beer is still a fishing village and the fishermen of Beer, like the men in these pictures *c.* 1960, fully deserve their reputation of unsurpassed seamanship. *Seaton Museum*

Above: Beer beach, *c.* 1895. *E.S. Gosling collection*

Below: Seaton from Haven Cliff, 1894. Note the absence of any buildings between Trevelyan Road and Beach Road. The house standing like a sentinel in the foreground was called the Watch Tower. This castellated dwelling, which stood at the end of Trevelyan Road, was the house of the preventive men (the predecessors of today's Customs and Excise). Trevelyan Road had been built across the back slope to give day visitors arriving by train quick access via a gate to the Explanade and beach. *E.S. Gosling collection*

The Undercliff, Beer, 1896. *E.S. Gosling collection*

View of Seaton Beach, *c.* 1897, showing the old West Walk which ran to Seaton Hole. *E.S. Gosling collection*

Extract from a 1904 guide to Seaton. *E.S. Gosling collection*

After the First World War the first visitors to the East Devon seaside resorts began to appear and here, sitting in low slung wooden deckchairs on Beer Beach during the summer of 1923, are two ladies enjoying the sun. *E.S. Gosling collection*

The new West Walk, Seaton, 1926. *E.S. Gosling collection*